Frontier Tales
Adventures in Choosing Right from Wrong

Let's Make Jesus Happy

By Mack Thomas

Illustrations by Bruce Day

Gold 'n' Honey
BOOKS

LET'S MAKE JESUS HAPPY

published by Gold'n'Honey Books
a part of the Questar publishing family

© 1993 by Questar Publishers, Inc.

International Standard Book Number: 0-945564-76-7

Printed in the United States of America

For information:
QUESTAR PUBLISHERS, INC.
POST OFFICE BOX 1720
SISTERS, OREGON 97759

93 94 95 96 97 98 99 00 01 — 10 9 8 7 6 5 4 3 2 1

CONTENTS

*For each of these twenty chapters, you'll find
"Questions to Talk About Together"
beginning on page 252*

Let's Make Jesus Happy

→ 1 ←

Over the Mountains

Buck Bannon was a happy man.
His wife Nelly was happy too.

Buck and Nelly always remembered
how good God is, and how great.
So God made them strong and brave…
and always ready for anything new.

One day,
Buck and Nelly and their three children
said goodbye to their friends
and neighbors and relatives.

Then the Bannon family traveled westward
over the great green mountains,
to build a new home in an unknown land.

After a long, tiring trip,
they came to a pleasant place
on the banks of a friendly stream,
and in the shadow of kind old mountains.

"Oh, Buck, let's live right here," said Nelly.

The children agreed: "Yes, Pa, let's do!"

And there the Bannon family stopped.

The children named the stream
Cherry Chum Creek,
because it was friendly
and gave them their water,
and because cherry trees
grew wild along its banks.

In one beautiful spot not far away,
the creek water flowed into a peaceful pool—
a great place to swim.
The Bannon children called this pool the Story Well—
because they loved to sit beside it,
to talk and tell stories.
They looked at their reflections in the water,
and listened to the sounds
of the dark forest all around.

Buck Bannon made a shelter for his family.
Then he began clearing away trees
to plant a cornfield,
and stacking logs
to build a real cabin for their home.

In the evenings
when the sun went down,
everyone was ready to rest
from the day's hard work.
If the children were listening,
they would hear their father praying:

"O Lord, please make my family happy here;
and help us all to make You happy, too."

⇢ 2 ⇠

A Warning

Soon the Bannons met new neighbors.
For not many miles away—
across three hills and two valleys—
was a village of the Tuckitaw tribe.

The chief of this tribe was a wise and noble man.
His name was Long-Look.

Chief Long-Look and the Tuckitaws
showed the Bannons the best places to hunt
and find food.

They showed them prancing deer
in the meadow they called Nanna-tunga.
They showed them proud buffalo
in the grassy valley they called Skona-toppa.
And they showed them jumping fish
in the river they called Chicka-lassee.

Chief Long-Look warned the Bannons
to be silent and almost invisible in the woods.
The forest could be dangerous, he said.

The Bannons knew there was danger
from bears and snakes and mountain lions.
But Chief Long-Look's warning
was about something else: about Wild Warriors
who sometimes came here from the far north
to trick people, and attack them.

The Tuckitaws had never heard about Jesus,
so Buck Bannon began to tell them about Him.
But it seemed as if Buck's words
were hard for the Tuckitaws to understand.

Meanwhile, Buck Bannon finished the log cabin
before the first winter winds blew cold.
He made beds and a table and chairs to go inside.

Buck & Nelly Bannon married in the sight of God, 1765. Their son Eli Bannon, born into this world 1767. Their daughter Rosabeth Bannon, born into this world, 1769. Their son Jonah Bannon born into this world 1772.

Each evening after supper,
by the light of the leaping flames
from the big fireplace at one end of the cabin,
Buck Bannon would bring out a big book.
And all the family would gather around him.

He would open the big book to the very first page.
And each night he would read aloud all their names
which were written there in fancy letters.

Then he would turn to other pages,
and read the words of God.
For this Good Book was the Bible.

Soon afterward the Bannons
would all go to bed.
They would fall asleep listening
to the crackle of the dying fire,
and sounds of the dark forest all around.

→ 3 ←

The Eagle Crest

Eli Bannon soon became good friends
with Red Vine, the son of Chief Long-Look.

Red Vine taught Eli many Tuckitaw games.
He also taught him many Tuckitaw secrets
about the woods and mountains.

Eli told Red Vine,
"Someday I want to be a Tuckitaw myself."

One afternoon Red Vine took Eli
on a steep and twisty trail
through the forest beyond the Story Well.

When they stopped climbing.
Red Vine pointed silently to a high cliff
rising up ahead.

"What is it?" Eli asked.

Red Vine slowly answered,
"That place is a secret place.
It is called the Eagle Crest.
The top is high,
where the eagles soar and scream.
Someday, I will go up there."

Eli was fascinated, and said, "So will I!"

Red Vine looked sternly at Eli and shook his head.
"Only the brave men of the Tuckitaw tribe
are allowed to climb the Eagle Crest."

Then Red Vine turned back to the cliff
with a question on his face.
"I don't know what they do up there.
They never tell anyone."

Words like this made Eli want to climb
the Eagle Crest even more. So he said,
"Red Vine, how close could we get?"

Red Vine thought about it.
"Tomorrow my father and all our brave men
will have a secret council up there.
As they climb, they may not mind if we follow—
if we are silent, and stay many steps back,
and if we stop before we get to the top."

Red Vine gripped Eli's forearm and said, "I will wait for you tomorrow morning at the Story Well. We'll climb together."

Then he added, "Be sure to tell no one."

⇢ 4 ⇠
A Scare

The next day, things didn't work out
as Eli wanted them to.

Very early, while it was still dark, his father left
with Molasses, the family's pack horse,
for a trip back over the mountain to lay in supplies
before the next winter.
He planned to be gone many days.

After breakfast, Eli's mother set out
for the Tuckitaw village, to do some trading there.
She left Eli in charge of his brother and sister,
and of all the chores the children needed to do.

As Eli watched his mother walk away,
he thought he would have to forget
about the trip he had planned with Red Vine.

But then Eli watched an eagle
soaring in the sky.

Perhaps it was flying
to the Eagle Crest.

When the eagle's shadow came over Eli,
he said aloud, "I've just *got* to go with Red Vine!
But how?" He knew he couldn't take
his sister and brother with him.
And if he left them at the cabin alone,
they were sure to get into trouble.

He saw Rosabeth and Jonah
playing in the clearing with Scrap,
the family's hound-dog.

Then Eli had an idea.

He went inside the cabin and came out with a rope.
He said to the children, "Let's pretend
I'm a Wild Warrior from the far north.
I'll capture you, and tie you up.
Then I'll pretend I'm a mountain man,
and I'll come to your rescue."

Rosabeth and Jonah let Eli tie them up.
"Not so tight!" Rosabeth said.
Eli tried to work fast. He hoped Red Vine
was still waiting for him at the Story Well.

When the last knot was tied, Eli said,
"If I'm a mountain man, I should climb
a mountain before I come to your rescue."
Away toward the woods he went.

Rosabeth decided she didn't like this game.
She began yelling: "Wait, Eli! A bear could get us,
or a mountain lion, or a real Wild Warrior!
Eli, come back!"

Eli shouted over his shoulder,
"Don't worry! You'll be fine!"

But just as Eli stepped out of the clearing
and into the shadows of the dark woods—
something big and alive leaped out in front of him!

Rosabeth saw it too, and screamed.

⇥5⇤

Strong Words

Eli stared up into the fearsome face
of a man who seemed twenty times his size.
The man's deep voice said slowly, *"Boy,
you have made someone MIGHTY UNHAPPY."*

Eli had the trembles all over.
He was afraid his knees
would shake out from under him.

Who had he made unhappy?…

Then he remembered
early that morning in the dark,
when his father was bending over his bed.
He had kissed Eli,
and said, "Goodbye, son.
Be brave and strong and good
while I'm gone."

"But Pa and Molasses
must be miles and miles away by now,"
Eli told himself.
"Pa can't be unhappy with me.
He can't even see me!"

Suddenly Eli heard again the booming voice
of the man who was blocking the trail:
"Boy, you have made someone VERY SAD."

What does he mean? Eli wondered.
And another memory burst into Eli's mind…

He remembered breakfast this morning,
when his mother was looking him in the eye.
She had said, "Promise me, son,
that you'll work hard today while I'm gone,
and that you'll take care of Rosabeth and Jonah—
in the same way I would."

"But Ma must be
across two hills and a valley by now."
Eli told himself.
"She can't see me either!"

Once again the big man's voice rumbled:
"Boy, you're not PLEASING someone."

Eli just couldn't figure out who that someone was.
So he stood straight and tall,
and said, "Who do you mean, sir?"

The man surprised Eli by suddenly bending low and kindly asking, "Don't your pa and ma ever read to you from the Good Book?"

Eli replied, "Yes sir, they do."

"And just who does that Book tell you about?" said the big man.

Eli knew the answer: "About the Lord Jesus, sir."

The big man slapped his knee with a loud pop.
"You're right as a rail! So tell me:
Were you making the Lord Jesus happy
by what you were doing just now?"

Eli hadn't thought of it that way.
"Making *Jesus* happy? *Me,* sir?"

The man laughed, and put both his huge hands on Eli's shoulders. "Surely you remember that the Good Lord watches everything you do. So do what's *right*, and you make Him *glad*; but do what's *wrong*, and you make Him *sad*."

The man stood,
took out his knife
and a whetstone,
and began
sharpening the
knife-blade.

He said calmly,
"You could try it.
Just ask yourself:
*What would make
JESUS happy—
right now?"*

So Eli tried it.
He asked himself the question.

And at once he knew a good answer.

→ 6 ←
The Mountain Man

Eli jumped around and ran to his sister and brother.
He untied them, and said, "I'm really sorry."

The big man followed Eli.

"Who are you, Mister?" Rosabeth wanted to know, after she was loose.

He answered,
"I'm a mountain man,
and my name is Jonah Bigg.
Topper is the name
of the cap on my head,
and I call my rifle Trusty."

With a smile, Rosabeth pointed to her little brother
and said, "His name is Jonah, too."

The big man picked up the boy in his arms
and said, "You're a big feller,
but let's call you Jonah Little,
just so nobody gets you and me confused!"

The children laughed with the mountain man.
Rosabeth continued the introductions:
"My name is Rosabeth Bannon,
and Eli is my big brother.
Pa's gone on a trip over the mountains,
and Ma's away for a while at the Tuckitaw village.
She left Eli in charge."

Jonah Bigg turned to Eli. "As the man around here,
Eli, tell me: What else would make Jesus happy—
right here and right now?"

Eli knew the right answer,
but his mind was still on Red Vine
and the Eagle Crest.
"Well sir, we've got chores to do…
but I know mountain men always have good stories
to tell! Maybe you could tell some to Rosabeth
and Jonah Little, while I take a walk in the woods."

Rosabeth's eyes grew wide, and she exclaimed, "Yes sir, tell us stories! Mountain man stories! Have you ever wrestled with a bear, Jonah Bigg?"

"Ohhhh, I can surely tell you stories about that," Jonah Bigg answered, with his eyes even wider than Rosabeth's.

"And I've swum flooded rivers,
and fought wildfires and windstorms,
and many a Wild Warrior too!
But I reckon you were right, Eli: It's our work
that will make the Good Lord happy right now.
Eli, if you and your sister and brother
will work your hardest, I promise to help you.
After that, we'll take turns telling stories."

With Jonah Bigg's strong muscles to help them,
all the children worked hard. Weeds were pulled
from the cornfield, the cabin was cleaned
and water buckets filled, and kindling wood was cut
and stacked in a neat pile by the fireplace.

It went so fast that Eli felt sure
Red Vine would still be waiting for him.

"Time for stories!" Rosabeth said,
when all the work was done.

Jonah Bigg asked, "Do you folks have a special place
where you like to talk and tell stories?"

"The Story Well!" Rosabeth exclaimed.

So the children led the way there.

➹ 7 ☙

Someone Hiding

Everything seemed quiet at the Story Well.
Eli saw no sign of Red Vine there.
But suddenly Jonah Bigg said softly,
"Someone is watching us."

The children froze in silence.

Jonah Bigg spoke again:
"Someone is very close;
I reckon it's someone
about your size, Eli."

The children slowly turned their heads
to look every direction, but they saw no one.

Rosabeth whispered, "Are you sure?"

Jonah Bigg raised one of his bushy eyebrows,
and answered her solemnly,
"For near forty years,
I've been tracking in the forest
for varmints of all sizes.
And I always know when I'm close.

"By any chance,
were you children expecting someone
to be here?"

Jonah Little shook his head no.
Rosabeth shook her head no.
And Eli shook his head no.

He told a silent lie.

Jonah Bigg's forehead became wrinkled, as he studied Eli for a moment. Then he pointed above his head and said, "Look straight up yonder."

The children looked, and there was a face, smiling from a tree-branch overhead.

"Red Vine!" said Eli.

And Jonah Bigg beckoned,
"Come on down and join us."

So Red Vine did.

Then everyone got quiet, as the mountain man began to speak.

→ 8 ←
Surprises for Red Vine

Jonah Bigg started with a question:

"Who's the wildest and wickedest warrior
the world ever knew?"

"The old devil," Eli quickly answered.

Then Jonah Bigg asked,
"Is the old devil a friend to Jesus?"

Rosabeth shook her head.
"No, he's a crooked enemy!"

"You're right as a rail, Rosabeth.
That's why when we make Jesus happy
it always makes the devil sad.
And when we make Jesus sad,
it always makes the devil happy."

Red Vine didn't know about Jesus.
So instead of listening to Jonah Bigg
and the Bannon children,
he began watching two butterflies
dancing in a circle.

Then Rosabeth thought of a question:
"Does *Jesus* make anybody happy?"

Jonah Bigg plucked a stem of grass
and twirled it between his teeth,
while he thought. "That's a dandy question,
Rosabeth. Eli, how would *you* answer it?"

"Well…" said Eli, while he pondered what to say.
"I think I would answer
that Jesus makes *us* happy…
and He makes God His Father happy!"

"You're thinking rightly," said Jonah Bigg.
"When Jesus—God's Son—came down to this earth,
He never ever did anything
to make His Father in heaven sad."

Red Vine stopped looking at the butterflies, and stared instead at Jonah Bigg and Eli.

Red Vine knew about God.
But he asked himself,
Does God really have a Son
who came down to this earth?
Red Vine had never heard of such a thing.

Jonah Bigg continued: "In fact,
one day Jesus was being baptized
in the Jordan River. Right then,
God sent down His Spirit from heaven.
He looked like a dove
flying down from the sunshine.
He fluttered low till He came upon Jesus.
Suddenly, like thunder,
God's voice called out,
'This is my Son, and I love Him,
and He makes Me happy.'

"Another day, Jesus climbed a mountain.
High upon that mountain, His face and His clothes
became brighter than the sun.
Once again, God's voice rumbled out like thunder:
'This is my Son, and I love Him,
and He makes Me happy.'

Questions raced through Red Vine's mind:
Can all this be true?
Is this Jesus the Son of God?
And is God really a happy God?
Does He smile and laugh?

Then Rosabeth said to Jonah Bigg,
"Will you tell us a mountain man story now—
about bears or wildfires or flooded rivers?"

"Don't forget," said Jonah Bigg,
"we agreed to take turns—and ladies go first.
Rosabeth, please tell us a story now
about something you've done
to make the Lord Jesus happy."

Rosabeth knew at once
the story she wanted to tell.

→9←

The Stranger

Rosabeth folded her hands in her lap,
took a deep breath,
and began her story this way:

"We have two cows — Mary and Martha.
In the daytime they graze
anywhere in the woods they like.

"But when the day is done,
we give them a handful of corn
and shut them in the shed
in the back of the cabin.

"They like that corn,
so they usually wander back home every evening
to get it — that is, *Mary* does.
But Martha usually forgets. It's my job
to go and bring Martha back from the woods.
She wears a cowbell around her neck
to help me find her. I like to practice my tracking,
and I sneak up on her as quiet as I can.

"Last evening, I thought I heard Martha's bell
a-ringing down in the hickory grove.
So I slipped through the woods in that direction.

"When I got closer,
I saw a strange man
leading Martha away."

Eli stood up with alarm.
"Rosabeth, you're making that story up!
You'll make Jesus sad if you don't tell the truth!"

"But I *am* telling the truth!" Rosabeth insisted.

"Then why didn't you tell Ma and Pa?" Eli asked.

Suddenly Rosabeth remembered why.
With dismay she said, "Oh, I forgot.
The man asked me to promise
not to tell anyone I had seen him."

Jonah Bigg quickly spoke up.
"Rosabeth, no matter what anyone says,
you don't *ever* have to keep any secrets
from your Ma and Pa.
What else did the stranger say?"

"First I asked him,
'What are you doing with Martha?'
He said, 'Oh, I saw this stray cow
and figured I'd take her to the closest cabin,
because we don't want the Tuckitaws to get her.'
Then he said to me,
'You hate those Tuckitaws, don't you?'
But I said, 'No sir, I don't,
because Jesus tells us to love everyone.'
Don't you think my answer
made Jesus happy, Jonah Bigg?"

"I reckon it did, Rosabeth,"
said the mountain man.
"But tell me: How did this man look?"

"Plumb awful," Rosabeth answered. "He had a mean face, and a scar above his eyes."

Now Jonah Bigg seemed alarmed.

"That man sounds like somebody I know.
His name is Tarbo, and he's a troublemaker.
He's hitched in with the Wild Warriors.
He hates people like you
who come over the mountains to live here.
So I reckon he wants to start a fight
between the Bannons and the Tuckitaws.
He's out to force you folks back
where you came from."

Jonah Bigg looked out in the woods
and muttered,
"Yep, wherever Tarbo goes,
trouble goes."

⇢ 10 ⇠

A Promise

Just then they all heard a voice calling—
it was the children's mother,
back from her trading trip.

Rosabeth and Jonah Little scampered away
to tell her about Jonah Bigg,
and about Tarbo and the Wild Warriors.

Red Vine gave a questioning look to Eli,
then walked silently into the woods.
Eli started to follow,
but Jonah Bigg asked the boy to stay.

"Eli, I reckon you and me
have something to talk about.
You were expecting Red Vine here, weren't you?"

While waiting for Eli to answer,
Jonah Bigg took out his knife,
picked up a stick, and began whittling.

Eli hung his head.
"Yes sir. I— I didn't tell the truth
when you asked us earlier."

The mountain man said sternly,
"It wasn't a *big* lie, but it *was* a lie.
I'm wondering if you can think
of any reason to be sorry for it?"

After a while, the boy answered:
"Yes sir, I can. I'm sorry for it
because I know it made Jesus sad,
and the devil happy."

Jonah Bigg spoke more softly now.
"Eli, if it's true that Tarbo and the Wild Warriors
are nearby, there's danger sure enough.
Since your pa's away for now,
you need to be a good, strong man
and help protect your family.
And a good, strong man never tells a lie.

"If there's trouble, Eli, I'm willing
to be your partner to help keep your family safe.
And I'll be your friend, too — but only if you promise
never to lie to me again. Will you promise?"

Eli put his hand in the big, outstretched hand
of the mountain man.

"Yes sir, I promise."

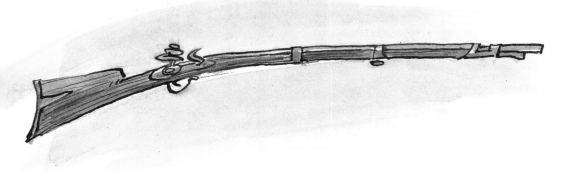

When the younger children came running back
with their mother, Rosabeth called out,
"There's the mountain man, Ma!
And his name is Jonah Bigg."

"Thank you, Mr. Bigg, for the help
you've given the children," Nelly said.

Jonah Bigg smiled. "You're right welcome,
Mrs. Bannon. I hope I didn't scare them too much
when I stepped out of the woods."

Nelly shook her head and replied,
"From what Rosabeth tells me,
we may have someone else to be scared of."

With a worried look, Jonah Bigg answered,
"I'm thinking I know this man Rosabeth saw
in the woods yesterday.
I'm afraid there could be a ruckus.
I'm only passing through here
from the river country out west,
but I'll scout around these parts long enough
to learn for certain what's going on."

"Before you leave, will you join us for some dinner?" Nelly asked.

Jonah Bigg answered, "I'm honored, ma'am, but time could be short. I'd best get out and take a look."

As he was leaving, Nelly called out,
"Mr. Bigg, we're all alone here now, and—
and if you think there may be trouble,
please come back and let us know."

The mountain man agreed to do just that.
Then he slipped into the woods,
silent as a big cat.

⇒ 11 ⇐
The Secret Council

Meanwhile,
at the secret council on the Eagle Crest,
Chief Long-Look and the brave men of the Tuckitaws
gazed into the sky.

Chief Long-Look prayed,
"O God-Spirit, do not forget us!"

Then Chief Long-Look spoke to his men
in the ancient Tuckitaw talk:

"Again I tell you old, old story.
It is story that Tuckitaws tell only in secret place.
We know not what it means.
But someday...we shall understand.
Then we shall be happy, and tell old, old story
to all our tribe— even to youngest child."

And this was the old story
Chief Long-Look told:

"Someday God-Spirit shall send
His Son to earth as man.
And how shall people know
this man is Son of God-Spirit?

"By these signs they shall know—
First sign: Bird come from heaven
and fly onto Son of God.

"Second sign:
Son of God climb high mountain.

"On high mountain, Son of God's face shine bright as noonday sun."

The Tuckitaw men
looked into the sky again
and asked the
Great God-Spirit
to show them
these signs…

and to show
them soon.

→ 12 ←
Troubling News

The next day,
Eli was pulling more weeds in the cornfield.

Out in the sun alone,
he was thinking what to do
if his family had to move
back over the mountains.

He told himself,
I'd rather stay here with Red Vine,
and become a Tuckitaw.

Just then he saw Red Vine stepping out of the woods.
Red Vine ran to Eli with important news:

"Tarbo the scar-faced man
was in our village today—with many
Wild Warriors! And he spoke with my father."

"What did he say?" asked Eli,
as a fearful feeling came over him.

"Tarbo said you people are enemies to the Tuckitaws.
He said we must attack you, and chase you
back over the mountains where you came from.
He said if we do not do it,
then he and the Wild Warriors will!"

"And how did your father answer him?" said Eli.

Red Vine smiled.
"I was glad to hear my father's answer.
My father said he would *never* attack you.
He said he would help you fight
against the Wild Warriors.

"Then Tarbo said to my father,
'Don't be so quick to answer.
Have a secret council tomorrow
with all your brave men.
Talk about it more,
and pray to your Spirit-God.
Whatever He tells you is right to do,
we also will do it.'

"So my father agreed.
Tarbo and the Wild Warriors went away.
They said they would come back in two days
to hear my father's answer."

With relief, Eli let out a big breath.
"That's good news, Red Vine.
Maybe everything will work out fine.
But if it doesn't, and if my family
goes back over the mountains—
I want to stay here,
and belong to the Tuckitaw tribe,
and be your brother."

Red Vine thought carefully before answering.
"You would be a good brother and a good Tuckitaw,
especially because you know
about Jesus the Son of God,
like the mountain man does.
But wouldn't it make Jesus sad
if you did not go with your parents?"

Eli felt he didn't want to answer that question
right then.

So Red Vine said,
"Eli, because your God is a God who smiles,
I would like you to tell me more about Him."

Just then,
they saw the mountain man Jonah Bigg
approaching the cabin to talk with Eli's mother.

"He must have more news," said Eli.

Red Vine nodded, and said, "You can go and listen, but I must go back now to my village."

As he turned to leave, Red Vine said,
"Eli, my father and the brave Tuckitaw men
will spend all day on the Eagle Crest tomorrow—
from sunrise to sunset.
Let's try again to follow them up there.
Come secretly to the Story Well at sunrise—
from there, we'll climb together."

Red Vine gripped Eli's forearm and added, "I won't go without you."

Then he vanished into the dark forest.

→ 13 ←

Another Promise

As Eli neared the cabin,
he heard Jonah Bigg speaking to his mother:

"Tarbo and the Wild Warriors
have been talking with the Tuckitaws, ma'am,
and I don't really know what will happen.
Stay on your guard, but I think we may have
a few days before there's any real danger."

The mountain man paused before he went on.
"I don't want to worry you, Mrs. Bannon—
but I have a snag in my mind about your husband,
out there alone in the woods.
If the Wild Warriors see him, well…
they may try something. I reckon I'll follow his trail
just to look for any sign of trouble.
If I don't see it, I'll feel certain he's safe."

Eli stepped closer. "Ma,
will Pa want us to move back over the mountains?"

Nelly took Eli's hands in her own.
"Only if he thinks it's right, Eli."

All the children gathered close to their mother.
Jonah Bigg said to them, "Stay right near the cabin
for the next few days. That will make your Ma happy,
and it will make Jesus happy too."

Then he looked directly at Eli
with eyes as deep as the Story Well, and said,
"Can you promise to do that for me, Eli?"

"I promise," Eli answered.

As Jonah Bigg started away,
Rosabeth smiled bravely and said,

"Hurry back with Topper and Trusty,
so you can tell us those mountain-man stories!"

➤14➤

A Decision in the Dark

Eli tossed and turned in his bed that night.

He couldn't forget his promise to Jonah Bigg.

But he wanted so much
to go with Red Vine at sunrise.
Surely there was some way he could do it!

He went outside the cabin
to watch for the light of dawn,
and to listen to the sounds of the dark forest.

He thought again how much he wanted
to be a Tuckitaw.

He wondered what would happen if his family
went back over the mountains without him.

Would it bring a smile to the face of his ma and pa?

And would it bring a smile
to the face of the Lord Jesus?

There in the peaceful night,
it seemed easy to pray.

So after a while, Eli said,
"Lord Jesus, I truly do want to make *You* happy…
even if it means moving away with my family,
and even if I never get to be Red Vine's brother,
or climb the Eagle Crest."

As the first light of dawn crept into the sky,
Eli made a decision: He would stay close to the cabin,
just as Jonah Bigg asked him to. And he would forget
about going with Red Vine at sunrise.

Suddenly, he heard noises.

Someone was coming near!

He ran inside the cabin, shut the door,
and alerted the rest of his family.

Out into the darkness
they looked,
and listened,
and waited.

→ 15 ←

Buck Bannon's Story

When the sounds came closer,
how happy Nelly and the children were
to see Buck Bannon
and Molasses
and Jonah Bigg!

Eli ran out to his father and said,
"Pa, will we have to move away?"

"No, son,"
said Buck Bannon with a smile.
"We're staying!"

Buck Bannon told everyone his story.

"On the mountain trail,
Tarbo and the Wild Warriors saw me alone,
and surrounded me.

"Tarbo said if I didn't agree
to move my family back over the mountains,
he would burn down our cabin and our cornfield,
and take us all prisoner to the far north.

"I said 'No, we won't go.'

"Then they took me and Molasses inside a cave.

"They tied us up to big rocks,
and left us there.

"As they were leaving,
I overheard their plans.
They said they would attack our clearing today,
while the sun is at the top of the sky.

I prayed mighty hard!
I figured there was nothing else I could do about it.

"But Jonah Bigg
is the best tracker in the forest,
and he found me.

"So now we must all get ready."

Then Buck Bannon looked up
and prayed for God to protect them all.

→ 16 ←

Wanting Help

Nelly Bannon got breakfast for the men
while they made their plans.

"We must have help from the Tuckitaws,"
Buck Bannon said firmly.
"Eli, run to the Tuckitaw village
and tell Chief Long-Look what has happened.
I know he and his men will come."

Eli suddenly shuddered. "Oh no, Pa!
Tarbo and the Wild Warriors have tricked us all!
Chief Long-Look and his men are away today,
and Tarbo knows it." Eli told his father all the news
that Red Vine had spoken yesterday afternoon.

Just then,
the first golden rays of the rising sun
came shining through the cabin window.

Eli saw this, and said,
"Red Vine is waiting for me
this very minute at the Story Well.
We wanted to climb together up the Eagle Crest,
to see what the Tuckitaw men do up there.
But after my promise to Jonah Bigg last night,
I knew I needed to stay here.
I knew it would make Jesus happy."

"You made a wise decision, Eli," said his father.

Jonah Bigg agreed. He looked at Eli and said, "Now your Pa and I should go with you, and talk to Red Vine."

Off to the Story Well they went,
hoping Red Vine could help them
reach Long-Look and the brave Tuckitaw men.

→ 17 ←

Two Volunteers

At the Story Well, Red Vine was surprised
to see Jonah Bigg and Buck Bannon with Eli.

The men told Red Vine
what the Wild Warriors were planning.

Jonah Bigg added,
"We must climb the Eagle Crest
and ask for your father's help."

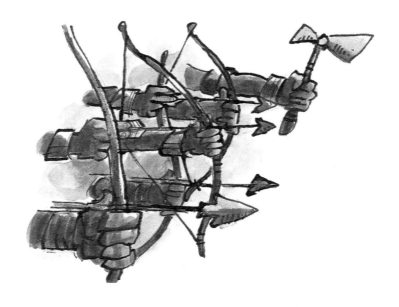

Red Vine said to the men, "You cannot go!
It is a secret place! It is only
for the brave men of the Tuckitaw.
They have arrows and tomahawks,
and they will attack you if you climb up there."

Eli knew that this would be Red Vine's answer.
Now he said bravely,
"They may not attack a young boy.
So I will go and talk with them!"

Immediately Red Vine said,
"I will go with you."

Buck Bannon saw the bravery in Eli's eyes, and smiled at his son.

"You have my permission to go—
and may the Lord watch over you, son.
Jonah Bigg and I will head back now
to guard the cabin."

At once,
Red Vine and Eli began the climb
they had wanted to make for so long.

→ 18 ←

A Life-Saving Message

At the top of the Eagle Crest,
the Tuckitaw men were very angry
when they saw the two boys.

They decided to tie them up
and throw them off the mountain.

Eli tried to speak up: "Chief Long-Look, sir,
I came to ask you for—"

"No talk!" said Chief Long-Look with a growl.
He reminded the boys that no one
except a Tuckitaw brave or chief
was allowed on the Eagle Crest.

"Unless," Chief Long-Look said gravely,
"you have message from Spirit-God."

Now Red Vine spoke up:
"Please, Father: Eli *does* have a message from God.
He knows about the Son of God,
who has come to this earth."

Suddenly the Tuckitaws became still and silent.

Chief Long-Look stared deeply into Eli's eyes,
to see if this was a boy who told the truth.
After a long look, the chief said,
"What do you know about Son of God?"

Eli slowly answered,
"Please, sir, if you untie me, I'll tell you."

After he was untied,
Eli talked about Jesus.
As he remembered the things
that Jonah Bigg told the children
at the Story Well,
he drew pictures in the dirt.

When he came to the part about God's Spirit
flying down like a dove upon Jesus,
the Tuckitaws muttered in amazement.

And when Eli told how Jesus climbed a mountain, and how his face became as bright as the sun, the Tuckitaws seemed even more astonished.

"Yes," Eli announced,
"this man Jesus is the true Son of God!
And *you* can make Him happy!"

As he said it, Eli could almost see
the smile on the Good Lord's face.

Chief Long-Look came closer to Eli.
"Please tell us more. Now!"

Eli answered, "There's much, much more
that my parents and I can tell you about Jesus.
But the Wild Warriors are attacking our cabin today,
and we need you there. Will you come and help us?"

At once the Tuckitaws were rushing down
to join the Bannons and Jonah Bigg at the cabin.
As he ran proudly with them,
Eli felt like a real Tuckitaw brave.

→ 19 ←

The Attack

Later that day,
Tarbo and the Wild Warriors
quietly approached the clearing
with their weapons ready.

Several of the warriors sniffed the wind.
What were those wonderful smells?

There in front of the cabin,
a feast of frontier food had been spread:
boiled corn and roasted corn,
bear meat and turkey meat,
jerky and johnny-cake,
apple-sauce and maple sugar…
and lots more.

Tarbo and the Wild Warriors came closer,
looking for Nelly Bannon and the children.

"Come out!" Tarbo ordered.

Nelly and the children came out.

"We've been expecting you,"
Nelly said with a smile.
"We'd like the Wild Warriors
to have dinner with us."

Tarbo was beginning to feel bewildered.
With a surly voice he said, "We're not hungry!"

Nelly kept smiling. "Oh, well, suit yourself.
But you aren't the only ones invited."

She turned toward the cabin and yelled,
"Time for dinner! Come out, everyone!"

Suddenly, out of the cabin came a stream
of Tuckitaws armed with tomahawks and bows,
plus Jonah Bigg and Buck Bannon with their rifles.

Tarbo and the Wild Warriors
stepped back in fear.

Jonah Bigg marched forward
and called out to the Wild Warriors:
"The Bannon family and the Tuckitaws
will not fight with each other.
And they don't want to fight with you, either.

"Instead," the mountain man said,
"they want to feast with you and be your friends."

Then Jonah Bigg pointed to Tarbo, and said,

"This scar-faced man has been wicked,
and he makes other people do wicked things as well.
He brings sadness to God.
You Wild Warriors are invited to share this food
with the Bannons and the Tuckitaws…

"But I will let *you* decide
if Tarbo should join us as well."

Hearing that,
Tarbo growled like a cornered bear.
Then the Wild Warriors suddenly
pointed their weapons at the scar-faced man.
That was enough for Tarbo.
He turned toward the woods
and ran away as fast as he could.

⇥ 20 ⇤

The Feast

Everyone enjoyed the great feast.
Meanwhile, Jonah Bigg and Buck Bannon
explained more about Jesus
to the Tuckitaws and the Wild Warriors.

When the Wild Warriors said goodbye,
they thanked everyone.

They said they would now go back
to the far north
and tell all the other Wild Warriors
what they had seen and heard.

Then everyone else went to the Story Well.
Jonah Bigg said, "In this water,
Buck Bannon and I will baptize anyone here
who wants to belong to Jesus,
and who wants to make Him happy everyday—
and forever."

Many of the Tuckitaws
were baptized in the water,
including Long-Look and his son Red Vine.

Chief Long-Look gave Eli
a thank-you hug, and said,

"Because you make God happy…
you make *us* happy."

Jonah Bigg stood on the edge of the clearing.
Waving goodbye to his new friends,
he said to the children,
"I'll be back someday to tell you those stories
about bears and wildfires and flooded rivers.
Until then, don't forget: Let's make Jesus happy!"

He waved again, and disappeared into the forest.

In the days and seasons that followed, the good friends Eli and Red Vine enjoyed their best times together.

And Red Vine often said to Eli…

"Now we are truly brothers."

Questions to Enjoy Together

1. Over the Mountains

- Why do you think Buck and Nelly Bannon are so happy?
- What did God do for Buck and Nelly?
- The Bannon children found a special place to talk and tell stories. Where is your favorite place to talk and tell stories?
- At the end of a day's hard work, what did Buck Bannon pray to God?

2. A Warning

- How did Chief Long-Look and the Tuckitaws help the Bannon family?
- What did Chief Long-Look warn the Bannon family about?
- What did the Bannon family do every night after supper?
- Why do you think we sometimes call the Bible the "Good Book"?

3. The Eagle Crest

- What did Red Vine teach Eli?
- Who are the only people allowed to climb to the top of the Eagle Crest?
- Why do you think Red Vine and Eli are such good friends?
- What do you like most to do with *your* friends?

4. A Scare

- Where did Eli's mother and father go?
- Why did Eli want to tie up his brother and sister?
- If you were there with Eli that day, what would you say to him?

5. Strong Words

- When we do something right, why do you think it makes Jesus happy? And when we do something wrong, why does it make Jesus sad?
- How can we learn more about what makes Jesus happy?
- What do you think Eli will do next?

6. The Mountain Man

- What kinds of things does a mountain man do?
- Why did Eli tell Jonah Bigg that he wanted to take a walk in the woods?
- How did the children get their work done so quickly that morning?
- If you could meet Jonah Bigg, what would you like to talk with him about?

7. Someone Hiding

- How do you think Jonah Bigg knew that Red Vine was up in the tree?
- What did Eli do wrong?
- What is a "silent lie"?

8. Surprises for Red Vine

- How does Jesus make *us* happy?
- When God called down to Jesus from heaven, what did He say to Jesus?
- How did Jesus make God happy?

9. The Stranger

- What is Rosabeth's job with the two cows?
- Why is Tarbo a dangerous man?
- What should we do if someone tells us to keep secrets from our mother or father?

10. A Promise

- Why is it wrong to lie?
- What does Jonah Bigg want to do now?
- What promise did Eli make to Jonah Bigg? Have you ever made that same promise to anyone?

11. The Secret Council

- What is the "old, old story" that Chief Long-Look tells to the Tuckitaw men?
- What do the Tuckitaw men want God to do now?

12. Troubling News

- Why do you think Eli would like to become a Tuckitaw?
- What does Tarbo want the Tuckitaws to do to the Bannon family?
- Red Vine asked a question that Eli didn't want to answer. What was that question?

13. Another Promise

- What is Jonah Bigg worried about?
- What promise does Eli make to Jonah Bigg?
- What does Jonah Bigg want to do now?

14. A Decision in the Dark

- Eli couldn't sleep that night because he was thinking about something. What was he thinking about?
- After Eli prayed, what decision did he make? Do you think this decision made Jesus happy? Why or why not?

15. Buck Bannon's Story

- What are Tarbo and the Wild Warriors planning to do?
- What are some things the Bannon family could do next in order to make Jesus happy?
- How can we tell whether we are making Jesus happy or sad?

16. Wanting Help

- Why does Buck Bannon want help from the Tuckitaws?
- How did Tarbo trick the Tuckitaws?

17. Two Volunteers

- Why can't Jonah Bigg and Buck Bannon go up to the Eagle Crest and talk with the Tuckitaws?
- If you were there that morning, would you also volunteer to go with Eli and Red Vine?

18. A Life-Saving Message

- How do Red Vine and Eli show that they are brave?

- Why are the Tuckitaws so interested in what Eli tells them?

- How is Eli making Jesus happy now?

- What are some things that you have told other people about Jesus?

19. The Attack

- Why do the Bannons and the Tuckitaws want to be friends with the Wild Warriors?

- Why do you think the Wild Warriors did not want Tarbo to stay at the feast with them?

20. The Feast

- What things about Jesus do you think Jonah Bigg and Buck Bannon explained to the Tuckitaws and the Wild Warriors?

- In what way are Eli and Red Vine brothers now?

- What is the very next thing you can do to make Jesus happy?